GARY CAYLOR

THE CONFIDENCE CODE

The Ultimate Guide About Building Self-Confidence, Learn the Effective Methods On How You Can Build and Master Confidence In Yourself to Win More in Life

Descrierea CIP a Bibliotecii Naţionale a României
GARY CAYLOR
    THE CONFIDENCE CODE. The Ultimate Guide About Building Self-Confidence, Learn the Effective Methods On How You Can Build and Master Confidence In Yourself to Win More in Life / Gary Caylor. – Bucharest: Editura My Ebook, 2020
    ISBN

GARY CAYLOR

THE CONFIDENCE CODE

The Ultimate Guide About Building Self-Confidence, Learn the Effective Methods On How You Can Build and Master Confidence In Yourself to Win More in Life

My Ebook Publishing House
Bucharest, 2020

GARY TAYLOR

THE CONFIDENCE CODE

book Publishing House
Bucharest 2020

TABLE OF CONTENTS

INTRODUCTION

Starting in the 1960s, the self-esteem movement in the USA and elsewhere began in earnest. The idea behind this educational movement is pretty straightforward. If you foster self-esteem in students, self- confidence will naturally follow. When people are more confident, they tend to excel better in life. This has been the accepted gospel in education policy for going on fifty years now.

The thinking is pretty straightforward. It's simply elegant, actually, since self-confidence involves one's attitude about one's ability to get things done. When people have a high opinion of themselves, confidence should naturally flow, right? Not quite.

It turns out of that "hollow" self-esteem only tends to produces impostor syndrome and, worse yet, and entitlement mentality. Whatever achievements people get with this mindset will be quite spotty.

In fact, in many cases, they are unable to replicate their earlier success. They tend to do things right from time to time but not all the time. There is no consistent threshold of success and excellence.

It turns out that the real solution to consistent victory still involves self-confidence; however, this self- confidence must come from the right place. It cannot be stimulated into existence through self-esteem.

Instead, you need to build your self-confidence on the solid bedrock of competence. Let me spell it out for you C-O-M-P-E-T-E-N-C-E. Put simply, you need to be the best you can be in something.

Anything. Find it. Do it.

Scale that upward spiral made possible by a feedback loop that you create. When you become competent in something, you become more confident. After all, you have shown to yourself that you can get things done. You can show up at the right time to produce the right things to achieve the right results with right people which then leads to the right outcomes.

This is not theory. This is not a guess. This is not something that just happened by random luck. This is something that you yourself made happen because you chose to be competent in something.

Once you see this play out, you become more confident. You start to believe that you can make things happen. What do you think happens next? That's right. The more confident you become, the more you do it and do it and do it.

This means that you do the things that you excel in different types of circumstances. You're able to overcome more challenges; you are able to solve more problems and you get better all around. When this happens, you become even more competent and, you guess it, even more confident.

So, this upward spiral process repeats itself over and over again. This is called a positive feedback loop. The more confident you become, the more confident you are, the more actions you take and the more opportunities you give yourself to get even better.

The bottom line is you need to start with competence. This fuels increasing levels of confidence. Competence is the linchpin to sustainable confidence.

Compare this to somebody who just got lucky. For whatever reason, somebody found themselves at the right time at the right place with the right people to produce the right results. So far, so good. That person racked up a victory for that day. Congratulations!

However, the next day, things simply did not line up properly. For whatever reason that this person can't quite put their finger on, things did not happen. The same thing happened the next day and the next day. Weeks turn into months, then what happens next?

That's right. There is no confidence there. Whatever confidence this person may have achieved because they got lucky or things just worked out that one day, is gone the next day or shortly thereafter.

Do you see how this works? Do you see the big picture? You need to build your self-confidence on competence because that's how you create an upward spiral system of positive feedback loops that enables you to become excellent.

In fact, you reach the point where you are so in-command of what you're doing that it doesn't really matter what you feel like. You can feel like a pile of crap the next day and still perform at a very high level.

People around you may be in a file mood but it wouldn't matter things. Things may not line up. All sorts of accidents happen. All sorts of unforeseen situations break out but, guess what? You're still able to perform at a very high level.

That's the difference between competence and confidence that flows from feeling right at the right time. In other words, that's the difference between competence and simply getting lucky. You cannot afford to get lucky.

Another thing about competence is that it is objective. If you go through that process of building up your competence one inch at a time, one step at a time, one block at a time, it cannot be taken away from you.

This book uses this interplay between competence and self-confidence to help you develop unstoppable confidence that can help you scale and overcome any kind of difficulty or obstacle.

CHAPTER 1

LET'S GET CLEAR FIRST!

Before we get ahead of ourselves, let's just get one thing out of the way. This is a fairly common issue. People trip themselves up on this issue. I don't want you to read this book and make this assumption.

Please understand that there's a big difference between self-confidence and self-esteem. They are not one and the same. Do not confuse these two concepts.

The Essence of Self-Confidence

Self-confidence is your attitude and your belief in your ability to get things done. This impacts your estimate of how likely you will succeed. This also affects how you feel when things don't go right. If you put this all together, it is no surprise that your self-confidence plays a big role in whether you're going to try an activity over and over again until you succeed.

Self-esteem, on the other hand, is all about your opinion of your value as a person. That's all it is. It is your esteem or your estimation of your value as a person, who you are, what you're about, what your capabilities are and what your capacities may be.

Two totally different things. Your self-confidence is about your ability. It impacts whether you are going to try something and how hard you're going to try. It also affects how often you're going to keep trying until you achieve a breakthrough. Oftentimes, it determines whether you're going to try at all.

Again, these are not one and the same. Do not confuse them. A lot of people think that as long as they fix their self-esteem, self-confidence will flow. I'm telling you that is the fatal logical flow made by the self-esteem movement in the United States.

We have so many people running around with a very high estimate of their worth as human beings. This is a good thing. I am not going to deny them that. However, the problem is this is a "hollow" assumption. They assume it coming in. It's kind of like a door prize. When they show up, they automatically put on the jacket labeled self-esteem. So far, so good, right?

Well, here's the problem. You can have a high view of yourself but that is no substitute for knowing the right thing at the right time with the right people to produce the right outcomes. Far from it.

You can think that you are the second coming of Albert Einstein but if you did not practice your quadratic equations and your calculus, you're going to flunk out on that test. This is not rocket science.

Sadly, a lot of people think that as long as they have self-esteem achieved through whatever means, they are going to get self-confident. They are going to be able to do things eventually. They have enough mental and emotional equipment to get things done.

Unfortunately, that has not been the case. Whatever success you may be able to achieve tends to be shallow, short-lived and unsustainable. You can't for the life of you achieve that same success the next day and the day after that. However, that's not good enough. As you probably already know, the world rewards sustainable ability to get things done.

The worst part of self-esteem is that it's subjective. I have value because I think I have value. I feel the right emotions. I feel good about myself. I can see myself doing all these things. I am somebody. That's great. That's awesome. It's definitely nice to hear, but you know what?

The world doesn't care about what you think. It couldn't care less about your feelings. What it pays attention to is what you do.

Can you do the job right, yes or no? Can you show up on time, yes or no? Can you do whatever it takes for however long it takes to achieve a certain result that needs minimal standards, yes or no? That's the level the world operates on. Everything else is noise.

Real Sustainable and Unshakeable Self-Esteem Must be Built an Object Reality

I've got some bad news for you. If you think that self-esteem is just something that somebody can give you because they say, "Try your very best", "I know you can do it", "You are special and don't you let anybody make you think otherwise".

Those are great words but the problem is if you buy into that hook, line and sinker, you develop hollow confidence. It's only a matter of time until that confidence starts to crumble like a brittle biscuit under the weight and pressure of reality.

Again, reality doesn't care about your feelings. Reality doesn't care how much time, effort and tears you put into something. When the test comes, you better come out on top. Otherwise, you fail.

That's all there is to it. It's black and white. Yes or no. Zeros and ones. It's a binary reality out there regardless of what other people tell you.

This is why real self-esteem must be based on competence. Competence is proven. Competence can be measured. Competence, most importantly, produces results.

CHAPTER 2

THE PROBLEM WITH MODERN SELF-ESTEEM

So, what is the problem with modern self-esteem? Why is it that a lot of people who have such high estimates of themselves tend to be mediocre?

In fact, psychologists have a term for one aspect of this personal overestimation. When it comes to our estimate of our ability to get things done and our general effectiveness, a lot of us suffer from the Dunning-Kruger effect. This is a cognitive bias that we have where we think we are superior in certain activities when it turns out from a purely objective test-based basis, we suck at them.

It is not unusual for people to share their opinions about weighty political and economic issues that they have absolutely no competence in. Whatever conclusion they come up with is obviously going to be defective and useless. However, that does not in any way prevent them from speaking up anyway.

The Dunning-Kruger effect doesn't just apply to online message boards, chat rooms and Facebook comments sections. It applies across the board. We tend to have a cognitive blind spot to the things that we suck at, but this is just a manifestation of the modern focus on exaggerated self-esteem.

In fact, a lot of us expect it to be some sort of door prize. It's not unusual for parents to say, "You are special, you are worthy, you are excellent" with absolutely no objective facts to back it up except, of course, with the kid's feelings. The lesson here is these parents are teaching their kids an unmistakable lesson. Your feelings stand in for reality.

It doesn't take a rocket scientist to figure out that this is a very dangerous idea. Again, you have all the feelings in the world and you could feel strongly. You may even be driven by the very best emotions and motivations, but none of that would matter if you can't produce results.

I hate to state an obvious truth, but life doesn't reward you just for showing up. There are no participation prizes in life. You have to hit certain minimal standards. You have to win at a certain level. You have to produce certain results.

This creates a hollow self-esteem. This type of self-esteem is very brittle. It only takes even the slightest disappointment for one person's self-esteem house of cards to come crashing down.

These people can't handle much of a challenge. If things get a bit tough, they're the first to pipe up and complain. They like to whine.

If you think that's rough, wait, it gets even worse. Simulated or fake self-esteem leads to an entitlement mentality. I'm sure you already know that life is not fair. I'm sure you've already gotten the memo that life can often be chaotic. You may have all the best-laid plans in the world, but the world just has a way of throwing those plans in the air.

You may have everything mapped out but, all of the sudden, something unforeseen happens. That's the way life is. It's chaotic. It's unpredictable, it's rough and it's unfair. In fact, it can be quite random.

Given this reality, the worst thing that you can do for yourself to assume an entitlement mentality. You show up and you expect things to be fair, easy, convenient and comfortable. What do you think you're setting up for yourself?

Again, it doesn't take a rocket scientist to see that you're setting yourself up for a life of frustration, discontent, unhappiness and a feeling that you are stuck in a world you did not create. You're not exactly setting yourself up for a comforting set of prospects.

CHAPTER 3

THE REAL FOUNDATION OF SELF-CONFIDENCE: COMPETENCE

What is competence anyway? Competence is your ability to get things done right.

It doesn't matter what it is. It can be an intellectual job. It can be something that you do with your hands. It can also involve your work process, showing up on time, putting in the work, making sure that work meets minimal standards, knowing what to do when certain conditions arise and knowing how to overcome challenges. This is competence.

Now, I'm not talking about excellence here. I'm talking about competence. You're meeting a standard of quality and, most importantly, you're able to do this day after day, week after week, month after month, year after year.

You're able to stick to that level of competence over an extended period of time. It's not something that you do when you feel like it. You're not a very competent person when you are hot and cold.

Competence is all about stability and you also must be able to ensure that your skill sets in whatever area in life stays relevant. You don't hang onto old skill sets that may have been valuable twenty years ago.

Let's get one thing clear. In the Internet age, as well as in the mobile age, skill sets that were valuable twenty years ago are almost absolutely worthless today. Competence is all about staying abreast of technology and keeping up with what's in demand.

How Competence Boosts Self-Esteem

When you notice that you are able to do the right things at the right time to produce the right results with the right people on a consistent basis, one realization kicks in. It's as if a diamond bullet hits you right in the middle of the head. You realize that you're not all that bad. You can actually get things done.

Now, you're not falling in love with yourself thinking that you're the best thing since sliced bread. It's not quite like that, but you get this calm realization. "I can get thing things done on a consistent basis. I can meet certain quality standards. I can do this all day every day".

You may be thinking that this is the most banal and innocent thing in the world. You might be thinking that this happens all the time. Well, there's actually a lot happening when you realize this. It all boils down to you realizing the power and impact of your choices.

You have to understand that the competent results that you have produced are unavailable to other people. They can't do it. How come? Well, at the root of it is that they simply do not make the right choices, but you can.

That's where your power comes from. You make a choice and you take action on that choice in such a way that the results of your choices meet a certain standard. It's all about your choice.

If you peel away the surface layer of that choice, it's all about your personal will. You could have made another choice. You could have avoided making a choice at all. A lot of people are good at that, but you made a choice by applying your personal will.

Competent people understand the connection between the choice that they make and the results that they get. The thicker and more defined that connection becomes, the more confident they become.

They understand that there is a strong correlation between them saying "I want this to happen" and then producing the results that they desire. Believe me there's something beautiful about being able to turn the ideas kicking around in your head, floating in varying degrees of definition and clarity into things that you could actually see, hear, touch, taste and smell. It's a beautiful thing. You create your reality when you do that.

Let me tell you there is no shortage of people who sit back and just daydream all day. They talk big. They talk about all the things that they could have done. They talk about things that could happen. They theorize about what they could possibly be doing, but not one of them is lifting a finger to make those amazing ideas reality.

You're not one of those people. You actually get up off your butt and do something about it. That's something to be confident about. That's something to feel good about.

Competence is not static. Competence is not some sort of label somebody puts on you. "You're competent" and just because they put that label on you, it magically transforms you

22

like Cinderella's fairy godmother transforming mice into men and pumpkins into carriages.

Competence is real precisely because competence is something you do. Competence shows not only the rest of the world that you can get stuff done, which is a big thing but it does something more.

Competence shows you your personal power and control.

There's a direct link between your personal will and your reality. This is the difference between guys who look at a Ferrari and say, "The rich are getting richer, and the poor are getting poorer, and I can't afford that car" and a guy who says, "What do I need to do to drive a car like that?"

When you ask yourself questions that trigger your imagination, creativity and resourcefulness, you start deploying your personal willpower towards a reality that you can manifest. Everything flows in that moment. You start looking at the outcome that you want, which is a Ferrari in your garage. Then you start coming up with goals.

How much is that Ferrari? How do I come up with $300,000? What kind of business activities can I engage in? What kind of sidelines can I put up? What is the potential ROI of these different sidelines? What are their advantages and disadvantages? What are their risks and rewards? What is the likelihood of success for each of these alternative options? What kind of resources do I currently have which is a better fit?

Do you see that line of questioning? Those come from people who get inspired by other people's success. They look at the fruits of success and it triggers in them a chain reaction of questions that ultimately result in actions that produce an outcome.

Compare this with somebody who just says, "I can't afford that". Case closed. Which would you rather be? I thought so. See you in Chapter 4.

CHAPTER 4

DEVELOP REAL SELF-CONFIDENCE
THROUGH COMPETENCE

One of my favorite cousins is a very, very confident person. He talks a big game He likes to brag. Sometimes he brags about stuff that most people wouldn't want to drag about, but that's my cousin. Every time I find myself in a room, he's always going to be the loudest person and you cannot miss him. You know that he's there. That's how big his presence is.

The problem is my cousin is very scary. He feels that whenever he works on a project, it will eventually fail. He's so afraid of failing that he'd rather talk about success rather than work for it.

This doesn't mean that I don't have a good time when I'm around him. This doesn't mean that I dislike him. In fact, it's the opposite. I have a really great time around him. I find his words inspiring, but I also know how to plug in the rest of the picture.

My cousin developed his self-confidence from a high level of self-esteem. I've already mentioned why this is a problem. If you want to be successful, you need to develop real self-confidence. This can only be achieved through competence.

I know it's uncomfortable. I know it's inconvenient. I know it would take quite a bit of sacrifice and time, but that's the way it is. This is the real deal.

You're not faking it until you make it. You're not engaged in some sort of group hypnosis where the more you project your self-image or self-esteem to other people, the more they bounce it back to you and you wallow in this artificial world that you create.

Unfortunately, such artificial worlds are like bubbles. It only takes one inconvenient challenge to blow up that bubble. You need to focus on developing the real deal, and this is real self-confidence built through competence.

The Benefits of the Real Deal

What exactly do you get developing self-confidence through competence? Well, first of all, your self- confidence will be sustainable. Even if you don't succeed the first time, the second time or even the first hundred times, you still will remain self-confident because you know that you are competent enough. So, you keep trying and trying until you succeed.

Now, compare this with somebody with a brittle self-confidence. It doesn't take much for them to lose harder. Even the slightest inconvenience, discomfort or challenge is enough to discourage them. In fact, they can get discouraged so quickly, so badly that they give up.

You have to remember success is a marathon. It is not a sprint. Sometimes, you get it the first time you try but, oftentimes, it's a long journey up ahead. You have to keep trying and trying and trying, and that's why you need sustainable self-confidence.

You can't just hit a snag and automatically start doubting your ability to get things done and eventually quit. That's not going to help you.

The real deal is also something that you trigger on command. When you're really confident about yourself, it is something that you activate on command.

It doesn't depend on things being right. It doesn't depend on how you're feeling. It doesn't depend on how other people around you feel. It doesn't depend on whether people are being supportive or not. It doesn't depend on any of that.

In fact, it is completely free of your circumstances and is based on something inside you. It is real precisely because it is resting on the hard, unshakeable foundation of competence. You've seen this happen before. You made things happen before. You can see with your own eyes the connection between your willpower and your ability to get things done. This is the real deal.

On-command self-confidence is your secret weapon. You can blow everybody away with this because you can perform at a moment's notice or at a snap of a finger. Other people have to wait for the circumstances to be right.

Well, I'm telling you you're going to wait forever because tomorrow never comes. You're just going to have to deal with reality as you find it right here right now.

Call Up Self-Confidence that Gets the Job Done ... Right

Another great thing about self-confidence based on competence is that you're able to get the job done the right way the first time around. Please understand that if you have the "hollow" self-confidence based on an inflated self-esteem, you can get stuffed up. Sure, from to time, you get inspired the right way. There are the right people around, they're seeing the right things and you're able to do it.

However, can you do it right day after day like clockwork? Chances are the answer is "no". Why? Again, you are dependent on how you feel. Did things line up the right way? Were you inspired properly? Did things just happen the right way?

Well, there are just so many things that you're dependent on for you to get the job done right. unfortunately, as I mentioned earlier, you're probably not going to get rewarded all that well if you're hot and cold.

Let me tell you the reason McDonald's is a fast-food giant is not because of the quality of their food. Okay? Let's get that out of the way. Maybe you're a big McDonald's fan or maybe not, but most people who have eaten more than their fair share of burgers will readily admit that McDonald's burgers are not the best-tasting burgers. At best, they are in the middle of the bell curve. Still, why does McDonald's make billions upon billions of dollars every single year?

Here's the secret. It may not be the best burger but regardless of which McDonald's branch you walk into, whether it's in Manila, Tokyo, Johannesburg, Paris, Los Angeles or Rio de Janeiro, you get the exact same taste and exact same quality. That's what people are paying for and expecting when they walk into a restaurant with those golden arches.

When you're competent, you perform at a certain predictable level. This ability is going to open many doors for you.

Compare a person who can perform like that with a person who may produce the very best work one day and then, for the rest of the month, flat out fails. That person is probably going to either remain stuck near the bottom or needs to get into a different field quickly.

If you are a writer, you can probably manage if you operate on that level. Maybe you only need to write one amazing novel and the rest would basically be mediocre, and you could still do well.

However, if you are in a field that requires a certain level of performance, and it may not be all that high, but you have to be consistent, then you have to be competent. This is what getting the job done right means. It's not just a question of getting the job done, but getting it done right consistently.

Sadly, people with brittle or hollow self-confidence may be able to get the job done from time to time or even get the job done excellently once in a blue moon. Unfortunately, this is not enough.

The Real Deal about Competence-Based Self-Confidence

If you develop this type of self-confidence, you develop self-confidence that cannot be taken away from you. It cannot be derailed. It is a product of your will, not your circumstances.

You become more persistent; you become more habitual and you become more courageous. You know that you already have it in you so it's a matter of just trying and trying and trying. Even if you are faced with really daunting challenges, you find the courage within you to try again and again and again.

You know full well that this self-confidence is rooted in your personality. It is not something that flows from your circumstances. It is not something that is a product of inspiration. It's something that you can call on demand.

CHAPTER 5

SETTING YOUR GAME PLAN FOR COMPETENCE-BASED SELF-CONFIDENCE

Now that you have a clear idea of what competence-based self-confidence is about, this chapter is going to step you through the five-step framework that you can use to develop this kind of self- confidence. Before we do that, please understand that there is no one-size-fits-all solution that works for all personalities, all people of all backgrounds at all times.

Don't even bother looking for that one-size-fits-all solution. It doesn't exist. It can't exist because we're all too different.

Instead, pay close attention to the five steps below as frameworks. This means that you can mx and match and modify, change, and tweak the different parts of these frameworks to fit your personal circumstances.

These are tools. They are not set in stone. You don't have to apply them lockstep.

What's important is you use these steps on your present circumstances and allow them to work with your present circumstances so you can make a change. That's what they're for. They have to bend to your situation, not the other way around. Don't expect that this is some sort of dictated set of rules that came from a mountain-top that will magically and/or mystically transform your life. It doesn't work that way.

You have to be in the mix. You have to actively work with this framework and adjust accordingly and make the right adaptations for them to work for you. Are we clear? Are we on the same page? Good. Here is the overview of the five-step framework.

Step #1: Find your existing areas of competence and pick one to improve

Step #2: Be fully aware of your increased competence and take confidence from it

Step #3: Use confidence from that one area of your life to empower and improve your competence in other areas

Step #4: Focus on mastery and control by letting your curiosity guide you

Step #5: Make sure there is no disconnect between your inner and external confidence

CHAPTER 6

START WITH SOMETHING YOU ALREADY DO WELL

The title of this chapter should be, at the risk of sounding grammatically incorrect and sending the wrong signal, start with something you already do well enough. The point is, you don't have to be the very best in whatever you're doing. If you like to swim, you don't necessarily have to be the next Michael Phelps. If you like to sing, you don't necessarily have to sing like Mariah Carrey. Just do it well enough.

The good news is, all of us on this planet have at least one thing that we are good at. Now, please understand that the word "good" is contextual here. It's comparative. This means that we do it "well enough." This is very easy to understand in theory, but for you to develop self-confidence based on competence, I need you to do the following exercise.

I need you to sit down and list out all the things that you think you are good at. Use a stream of consciousness method. In other words, the first thing that comes to your mind, write it down. Ask yourself this question: What am I good at? What do I do well?

So, write it down. No need to edit yourself. No need to second guess yourself.

If you think that's it's partially or even has a chance of being accurate, write it down. Get a massive list going.

Go through your list and actually do these activities

Now, this is where it gets tricky. I want you to actually do these activities. It will probably take some time. It's very important that there are other people giving you some sort of assessment. Maybe they're clapping their hands. Maybe they're looking at you. Maybe they're raising their hands. Whatever the case may be, there has to be some sort of objective feedback. These are your results.

Ideally, you should be getting a grade or you should be getting money. Whatever you do, there has to be some sort of feedback mechanism. This not just you sitting down by yourself and chuckling about the idea that you're good at Fortnite. There was to be some sort of objective standard out there.

Again, you're not expecting yourself to be very best or a world class standard. There just has to be some sort of measurement of external results. Write down these results and rank them.

Identify and slice and dice

By this point, you should have a fairly clear idea of the things that you do reasonably well as measured by objective results. You're not just going by your subjective impression here. You're not just going by your own personal opinion of how well you do. There is some sort of objective feedback here.

Now, slice and dice them. What I mean by this is you'd look for the top 5 or top 6 and then get rid of everything else. Next, you slice and dice the things that you do well. When you do something, it has many different components.

For example, if you are good at public speaking, then this means that you have to have a script, you have to have some sort of preparatory steps, you will speak, you will use body language, you will use voice modulation and you will use the right facial expressions. You might even make gestures.

When you dissect the activity into these different parts, you slice and dice it. You figure out which parts account for the results that you're getting. Now that you have done this for the

36

five to six activities that you objectively get good results with, pick one that has the most parts that get the most results. You won't be able to figure this out unless you slice and dice them.

Systematically improve

Now that you've broken down that particular activity in the different parts, improve the parts that require improvement. I've got some good news for you. Most people will have areas for improvement. In fact, chances are, you're not going to perfect across the board. So, look for those parts and improve them by constantly practicing or acting them out with an eye towards improving that particular section.

Make predictions on how this tweak or modification can lead to improvements. Make sure you measure improvements based on the actual external results that you get. If you do this, then you should be able to create an upward spiral of improvements. What do I mean by that? Well, you will break down what you're doing and then you can decide what you're going to do to improve it.

You make a move and if you see the improvement, you feel better about it. Then you try it some more and you do a better job and this leads to you trying more, acting more and getting better and better results. Now, please understand that this can go up and down, but generally speaking, the pattern should trend upwards.

Focus first on subjective improvement

Now that you have a clear overview of the improvements that you're going to make, here is the nitty- gritty of the improvement system. The first thing that you're going to do is you're going to focus on the subjective elements. You have to have a positive view of the results that you're getting.

Deep down inside, you're thinking that you are making an improvement. You feel it. It makes you feel good. It makes you feel like you're somebody.

Shift to objective results

Now this is where the rubber meets the rubber meets the road. Great feelings and emotions are awesome and everything, but at the end of the day, the world only rewards results so we're going to have to shift to objective results. Look at the results that you're getting. Are people clapping more? Are you getting paid more? Are you getting a lot more attention?

I'm talking about qualitative here. This is something that you can reduce into writing, something that you can boil down into a number, not just feelings or hopeful expectations. It's important to make sure that you quantify the results you're getting. Can you see it?

Now, how do you "see" objective results? First of all, you need to ramp up output. For example, you're trying to become a better employee. Previously, you were only able to produce one report a day at your research firm. Apparently, this is enough not to get you fired, but as you probably already know, that's not enough to get you promoted or get you a raise.

When you shift to objective results, the first thing that you're going to look at is to measure your improvement based on how you ramp up output. If you stay stuck at one report a day, you're not making progress. I don't care how good you feel. I don't care how awesome you think you are. It could be just that Dunning-Kruger effect.

You're not all that competent but you think you are the best thing since sliced bread. Not good. You have to be able to show these objective results. The first hurdle that you're going to have to clear is output. You know you're going in the right direction if you are now cranking out two research reports. Congratulations, you have made a 100% improvement.

But don't stop there. See if you can hit three, then four, then five. I know it sounds like a tall order, but let's get real here. If you are to boil down all actual productive work you do in the span of an 8-hour work day, chances are you're clocking it at maybe one hour if you're lucky. The rest is basically checking emails, social media updates, talking to people at the water cooler, you name it.

There is definitely a lot of space and resources to work with if you choose to be completely honest with yourself, so five reports per day may not be asking for too much if you are going to fully apply yourself. That is the first hurdle. You're going to shift to objective results in terms of output. That's the first way you know you are making progress.

Keep hitting output. See it scale up. Next, you have to scale up quality. I'm telling you, crap times 1 million is still crap. Crap is not going to get you that corner office. It's not going to get you a substantial raise. It's not going to get you much respect. If you duplicate something that isn't very good millions of times over, people are not going to be all that happy, so scale up quality.

You are already scaling up output. You have to scale up quality. When you pair this up with subjective improvement, your feelings about what you're doing improve as well. It becomes clear to you that you are making progress and this gives you an objective basis for competence. You're not just feeling this. You're not just imagining this. This is real.

CHAPTER 7

ALLOW YOUR OBJECTIVE COMPETENCE
TO BECOME A PART OF YOU

As I mentioned earlier, the Dunning-Kruger effect is a serious problem. It leads to all sorts of funny and not so funny results and situations. Unfortunately, a lot of people who are otherwise competent tend to compartmentalize their competence. They think that they are very good at packing boxes at a factory, but that's at the factory. That's just one part of them.

In the big scheme of things, that area of competence really isn't all that important, so what do you think happens? These people have low self-confidence, low self-esteem and they have a fairly bleak picture of who they are as a person, what they're about and what they're capable of doing. Sad, but all too common.

They're too quick to dismiss or diminish their areas of objective competence. I can't even begin to tell you how many people that I've met who are really good at one area of their life or one section of their work, but for the rest of their lives, they feel that they suck and they let it eat away at them. It really is quite sad.

Well, the point of this book is to use areas of competence to give you genuine sustainable self- confidence. You're going to have to destroy that tendency to compartmentalize. How?

Celebrate your objective competence

The first thing that you need to do is to understand in full emotional terms that you're looking at something real. Your competence in packing boxes, writing reports, dictating articles, transcribing, writing books, doing data entry or what have you, is real. You do a good job on them.

How do you know? You produce a certain output and you can see the quality of the work that you do. This is objective. This is not just happening in your head. You can tell from the objective results that you get. You're not just dealing with the opinions or estimations of yourself.

Now that you realize that this is objective, real and supported by external feedback, think about it some more. Think about your objective results more. Focus on the number. Think to yourself, I used to do only one, now I'm doing two or three. My output used to be full of grammatical mistakes, now my stuff is smooth.

Whatever the case may be, wrap your mind around your objective results. Let it sink in. Be as clear as possible regarding the quality that you are able to achieve.

Feel good about your objective results

Let it sink in so much that it feels good. Tell yourself this truth: other people can't do this. If you're a writer and you are writing or dictating 10000, 20000, 100000 words a day, few other people can do that.

After all, a lot of people think writing is a hobby. They'll get to it when they can get to it. You, on the other hand, crank this stuff out regardless of whether you feel like it or not. Regardless of whatever else is going on in your life, you are able to do it on time, every time. That's something to feel good about.

If you work at a factory and you meet quota every single day, that's something to feel good about. How come? Well, your boss probably holds meetings about the fact that a significant portion of the workplace cannot consistently meet quota.

If you're a businessperson, the fact that you are able to close a certain number of sales every month is something to feel good about because not all business people are able to do that. In fact, a lot of businesses struggle because of peaks and valleys in their sales volume.

Find something to feel good about your objective results. Again, these have to be objective. These have to be reduced to numbers. These are not lies, opinions or estimations. These are your objective results. Feel good about them. Keep repeating to yourself, "Not everybody can do this."

For example, if you are a writer that dictates your books, articles and blog posts, not everybody can look at two sentences and dictate a whole book out of that. Celebrate what you've got going for you. If you are a person who transcribes, not everybody can get the context of what the speaker is saying and transcribes it in such a way that captures the essence of the passage.

Pat yourself on the back. Not everybody can do what you're doing. In fact, the more focus you put into your craft, the more sunlight you put between you and the next person. That's how good you are.

You're special.

Talk about your objective results

It's one thing to feel good about your objective results. It's another to actually talk about it. Tell your friends about your work, what you do and the things you're able to do. Now, please understand that how you say things is just as important as what you have to say.

You don't want to come off as some sort of blowhard.

You don't want to beat them up with this information, but be proud of what you do. Talk about the details of your job so people can say, "Okay, you know certain things that I don't." If they're really your friends, they would be interested. This would be fascinating to them because they do the same to you.

Let your positive estimation or opinion of the objective results that you're getting in one area of your life change the way you talk.

Focus on a sense of mastery and ownership

If you change the way you feel and talk about the objective results that you are getting from one area of competence, you start changing your mind about it. You no longer compartmentalize it. You're no longer dismissing it as one part of your life that doesn't really mean much of anything. Instead,

45

it becomes clear to you that at least in this particular area of your life, you're getting a sense of mastery and ownership. This is a big deal.

Now you are making serious progress. You're not longer looking at that item as an empty detail that is just part of who you are. No. Instead, it becomes a source of objective validation of the fact that you can take ownership and mastery over your life.

Right now, it might be a faint glimmer. The outlines may not be all that well-defined, but you sense that it is there. This is objective. This is real.

Allow yourself to be confident

Once you're able to focus on a sense of mastery and ownership, confidence naturally flows. The moment you realize these two things, you start saying "I can" statements to yourself. I can make things happen that meet a certain standard. I can overcome challenges consistently. I can decide and things pan out based on my choices and ideas.

If you can't feel confident about these statements, just wrap your mind around the fact that a lot of people cannot make these statements. In fact, these statements don't even occur to them. They just focus on making it to the next day or they're just focused on the big victory that they are hoping in vain for. They don't focus on the areas of competence they already have.

Repeat this to yourself: I can, I can, I can. The two words in that phrase celebrate your individuality, your ownership of your reality and your power to assert your will over your reality. Big stuff. Heavy stuff. Real stuff.

Act confidently more often

In the previous steps, you're feeling good about your objective results. You're talking about them. Deep down inside, you hear this echo of "I can, I can, I can." This is all great, but like I keep saying in this book, the world doesn't care about your feelings. That's right. Your emotions are just like everybody else's emotions, meaningless.

The world pays attention to what you do, so you have to translate all that "I can" into acts of confidence. Act confidently. I repeat it again and again, act confidently more often. Keep increasing competence in your target area. Nail it. It can be an inch wide, but boy, you need to make it miles deep.

The more competent you become, the more confident you get. The more you repeat "I can," the higher your estimate of your ability to get things done according to your will. The more confident you get, the more challenges you take on. This is very important. Real confident people don't just sit back and say, "Oh, I can do that, but I'm not going to do it." No, you're just fooling yourself. You're just a blowhard.

Real confident people look at challenges as a way to build up their competence. They know what they're about. They look at challenges as opportunities. It doesn't scare them. People who are just blowhards, arrogant or people suffering from brittle self-esteem talk a good game. They talk big. But the moment the challenge appears, they get scared. They run away like little boys.

You, on the other hand, look at the challenges and stare them straight in the eye and take them on because you know that they are opportunities. The more of these you take on, the more likely you will succeed. Now, please don't get me wrong. The first few times, you'll probably fall flat on your butt.

That's just the way things are.

You only need to look at the time when you first learned how to ride a bike. Chances are, you probably did not get it the first time around. But you kept trying and trying until eventually you were able to bike away. The same applies to these opportunities.

The more problems you solve, the more competent you become. The more competent you become, the stronger that "I
48

can" statement becomes and your estimation of what you're capable of increases tremendously. Keep repeating the process above because it creates an upward spiral. The more competent you become, the more confident you become. T

The more you try things which leads to even more competence and even more confidence, and on and on it goes.

CHAPTER 8

TAKE OWNERSHIP OF MORE AREAS
OF YOUR LIFE

Once you have achieved the positive feedback loop in one area of your life, you become really confident in that narrow part of your life. Again, it doesn't matter if it's just an inch wide and a mile deep. That's okay as long as you get that positive feedback loop going and as long as you really feel deep down inside "I can. It's not just possible, I do it."

If you're able to let this sink in and it becomes a part of you, you don't become a blowhard. You're not that guy who's basically out to prove to other people who he is, not somebody talking big who has got something to prove. Instead, you develop an easy, calm, self-assurance over at least one area of your life.

When you look around you and you see people doing well, talking big, enjoying themselves, you say to yourself, "You know what? I have one area of my life under control because I can make things happen there," and you gain some self-assurance. You're not banging a gong, saying, "Hey, look at me," but the confidence that you get flowing from that area is real. It burns. You can call it on demand like a personal genie.

Apply your ownership mastery mindset to the next most competent area of your life

In a previous exercise, you listed up the things that you are competent at. Go to #2. You started out with #1, now let's go to #2. Check back with your stream of consciousness list items and go to #2. Repeat what you did in Chapter 7. The bottom line here is action.

Act confidently more often

Keep increasing competence in that target area. The more competent you become, the more confident you get. The more confident you get, the more challenges you take on. These challenges, when properly viewed, are opportunities. Maybe it's an opportunity to learn how to deal with defeat. Maybe it's an opportunity to learn how to deal with being told to wait or to handle rejection.

It takes many different forms, but they all lead to the same place. They all lead to mastery if you allow them to. The more problems you solve, the more competent you become. Keep repeating this process above. You started out with an area of your life that is an inch wide and you get to the next one, so now you have two inches wide that you're dealing with and that you have attained mastery over.

Then you move on to the next area and then the next. This is how you take ownership of more areas of your life.

CHAPTER 9

UNDERSTAND THAT SELF-CONFIDENCE CAN BE LIMITLESS

It's really important to understand that competence has limits. You may be a good swimmer. People might think that you are awesome, but let's get real here. Chances are quite good, you're probably not going to be the next Michael Phelps. Guess what, it's perfectly okay. Competence has limits and that's fine. Just allow it to give you what you're looking for, which is self-confidence.

You're not looking to be the very best. You're not looking to be the next Usain Bolt or the next Stephen Hawking. Instead, you just have to push yourself to the point where you say, I did it. I started here, now I'm up here. This means that I've overcome my fears, I wasn't complacent, I pushed myself, I applied myself and now I have something to be proud of. I have something that I can take confidence in.

The secret to competence

Although competence has its limits, self-confidence doesn't. If you think about this, the interplay between competence and self-confidence, this means that competence can be limitless as well. How? Well, while confidence can be limited by your circumstances, if you let yourself be motivated by curiosity and your sense of possibility and adventure, the sky is the limit when it comes to your confidence in getting things done.

In other words, you think to yourself, I know that I am a good businessman. I can build businesses and I can sell them, but I can also deal with setbacks. If there was a stock that crashed tomorrow, I can deal with it. If you develop that kind of self-confidence, the sky is the limit.

All bets are off in terms of your competence because, again, your competence is linked to your self- confidence. The more competent you become, the more self-confident you become. The more self- confident you become, the more you do things and you figure things out. This leads to even more competence and even more self-confidence. It's an upward spiral.

Self-confidence can be limitless. Take confidence in this. Feel good about it. How? Celebrate and seek out greater mastery

Self-confidence can be pushed, but it cannot be developed just by you sitting back and bragging, thumping your chest, parading around like a peacock. No, it doesn't work that way. To boost your self- confidence, celebrate your current mastery, but seek out greater mastery. How? Test your versatility, your sociability, your adaptability, your imagination and sense of possibility.

This also means testing and pushing to the limit, your perseverance, tenacity and grit. Grit is a big deal because according to a research by Prof. Duckworth based on her studies of different cohorts. While people may vary based on their IQ and ability to socialize and other measures of emotional intelligence, grit, party defined as tenacity, is one trait that pretty much unites people who come out on top.

They might not be able to get to the top tomorrow, but they will eventually get there. If you're using this interplay between competence and self-confidence, grit must be part of the equation. How do you develop grit? Well, it means you take more risks. The more risks you take, the higher the chance that you will fail. Instead of running away from failure and loss, you actually view it as an opportunity because that is what builds grit.

Success doesn't build grit. Having things play out the way you had expected and hoped doesn't build grit. Loss, failure and the risk of shame, humiliation and ridicule, those build grit. When you look at all of this is totality, you see that nothing can get you down. Even setbacks can be victorious. How is that for unstoppable self-confidence based on the solid bedrock of competence?

CHAPTER 10

MAKE SURE THERE IS NO DISCONNECT BETWEEN YOUR INTERNET AND EXTERNAL CONFIDENCE

One thing I noticed about people with brittle self-esteem is the fact that they actually have a disconnect between their external confidence and their inner confidence. A lot of people have estimations of themselves, but they're also not stupid. They can see that they suffer from the Dunning-Kruger effect.

They think that they are the best thing since sliced bread. But the moment they step up and try to get results going, they fall short. They're not dumb. They know that there is this disconnect between how highly they think of themselves and their abilities and what they're able to achieve and their results. At best, they are mediocre.

What happens then is that there is a distinct break between the confidence that they project, which is still very high and can still open a lot of doors and set the people at ease and get the ball rolling.

Unfortunately, this is paired with a dubious inner confidence. Their confidence wavers. It doesn't feel quite right. It can't quite make up its mind. It can be very flighty.

This is just one manifestation of the disconnect between internal and external confidence. Be aware of this disconnect and its many different forms.

The ever-present imposter syndrome

I had a business associate in the past who was a very successful Kindle author. This person's books on Kindle sell really well. He easily makes six figures year after year. Unfortunately, he thinks he's the biggest fraud in the world. He outsources his books to third party ghost writers. He basically does the research and he lets the writers flesh out the books, which he then publishes under his name.

I talked to him about this and I said to him, "What you're doing is really not much different from what big name authors do. I can count with many fingers, big name self-help authors who use ghost writers.

It's the best kept secret in the industry." But this person still thinks he's a fraud. This is called the Impostor Syndrome.

These people are very competent. Let me tell you, 99% of other Kindle authors in his niche or his genres can't hold a candle to what he does. Sure, he doesn't write his own stuff, but he shapes the books. He applies his own distinct personality to them. He edits key parts. They become part of his brand.

This brand did not come out of nowhere. He wasn't handed this author platform. He had to write his own books himself before he started making good enough money to outsource the rest of his publishing empire. That is competence.

Unfortunately, if you suffer from a disconnect between your internal and external confidence, Impostor Syndrome is one of the symptoms. It can be very debilitating. In fact, if you don't deal with it, it can lead to all sorts of nasty self-fulfilling prophecies.

Focus on objective results first

The key to solving any kind of disconnect is to focus on objective results first. Can you get the job done? Are you a bestselling author or not? Are you at the top of your law school class or not? Are you at least in the top 10%? Did you write a medical report that gets the job done or not? Focus on these black and white objective results first.

This goes a long way in getting you to focus on what you should be focusing on, instead of just letting your feelings get the better of you. Let's face it, they can run riot. They can be all over the place as far as your feelings go. Competence, on the other hand, is objective. It can often be reduced to black and white.

Internalize the intensity of your objective results

Now that you can see just by looking at your bank account that you can get stuff done at least when it comes to business or when you look at the beautiful women you come with every time you go to a social gathering, internalize these results. I know you may be feeling at some level or other that you are an impostor.

You may be thinking to youself, why is this hottie going home with me?

I'm a totally abject failure and loser. Displace that inner monologue by internalizing the intensity of your objective results. You're doing something that most guys which they could do, okay?

The fact that you can go home with a woman that looks exactly like Kate Upton is a victory in of itself because most guys cannot achieve what you're doing. You just met her and now you're going home with her. Take the win.

Live a life of total emotional and psychic integrity

Now, integrity is a big word, but the integrity I'm talking about here is the alignment between your internal and external confidence. You have to line them up. You can't just say you're the biggest fraud or impostor in the world, you feel crappy, but you are very competent. They have to line up because this is the key to unleashing even more powerful waves of confidence that leads to such better results.

Again, this is an upward spiral and this is not just limited within that inch wide and miles deep segment of your life or several of them in your life. I'm talking about across the board.

Confidence is something you do

I know I've said this before, but confidence is something that you do. What exactly does it do? Confidence enables you to project your wishes to the world. I wish to be a contract poultry farm owner. I wish to become a bestselling Kindle author. I wish to become the best mother I can be. There are many things you can project out, but confidence enables you project clearly and then do them.

The more you do it, the more confident you become and the more things fall into place. It's not going to be smooth. Don't expect to hit a home run the first time you swing that bat. But the more you do, the more opportunities you give yourself to be competent. This leads to you thinking that you are more and more and competent.

This changes what you say, which again leads to you improving what you do. Real confidence is not the following

Let me tell you, real confidence is not bragging. I can't even begin to tell you how many dinner parties I've gone to and sure enough, it's usually the loudest person there that has the least money, gets the least action, drives a very fancy car with only $5 in gas, is up to his or her neck in debt, you name it.

Real confidence is not bragging.

If you are truly competent, you keep it to yourself. The results speak for themselves. You're a cut above. Real confidence is nothing to bang a gong about. There's no need for that because you're playing for an audience of one. You know you can get things done. There's no need for you to whip out a Hermes bag or parade around in Prada or Armani.

You can if you want to do that. That's part of your personality. But in terms of reminding yourself of your confidence, you don't need to go there. You can leave the bombast at home. Real confidence, in turn, is calm, assured and self-controlled. In fact, the more you take control over it, the less you feel the drive to let everybody know that you are competent and confident.

Just think about it. Even if everybody thinks you're the best thing since sliced bread, that's not really going to help you because deep down inside you know that you suck. We're not dealing with group hypnosis here. Real competent people know what they're about and they couldn't care less about their circumstances because their circumstances did not make them.

Other people's backslapping, compliments and favorable descriptions of you do not make you. You made yourself. That's real power.

Printed by Libri Plureos GmbH in Hamburg, Germany